PORTRAIT OF
SHROPSHIRE
&
THE MARCHES

VAN GREAVES

HALSGROVE

First published in Great Britain in 2005 as *Moods of Shropshire & The Marches*
This edition published 2008

Title page photograph:
Caer Caradoc from The Wilderness

British Library Cataloguing-in-Publication Data
A CIP record for this title is available from the British Library

ISBN 978 1 84114 837 3

HALSGROVE
Halsgrove House
Ryelands Industrial Estate
Bagley Road, Wellington, Somerset TA21 9PZ
Tel: 01823 653777   Fax: 01823 216796
email: sales@halsgrove.com
website: www.halsgrove.com

Printed and bound by
Grafiche Flaminia, Italy

Introduction

Shropshire, a superb county of pictorial contrasts, has its obvious boundaries shown on the map. The term 'The Marches', however, is a conception, perhaps invented because of the numerous dog-legs of the Welsh border, whose wanderings make it almost impossible to define the changeover from English to Welsh territory. Not only that, it is also difficult to geographically and geologically separate it from parts of Herefordshire. Hence, the 'back of beyond' mystique of the Marches; quiet, unspoilt hill country, where walkers may travel all day and not see another soul.

Consequently, for the photography of this book, I have made arbitrary forays across the Welsh border and into Herefordshire, where English names spill over into Wales, and Welsh-sounding names back into Shropshire and Herefordshire.

The Clee Hills are Midland sentinels guarding hill country which continues west to the Welsh coast. To these Shropshire hills, add Caer Caradoc, the Long Mynd, Stiperstones and Corndon Hill among others. Beyond, they ripple out to the Clun Hills, and places of wilderness, high arable fields, plantations and many hill forts dating from the Iron Age.

Another ancient borderline feature is Offa's Dyke. While not finding truly mountainous features, a walker on the the long-distance path which now follows this route will certainly get to know about its many ups and downs.

The Marches stretch south to the Black Mountains, and north to the Llangollen hills. North Shropshire is generally flat with endless arable fields. There are meres (lakes), canals, fine towns, historical villages and homes and the 'Cradle of the Industrial Revolution' beside the Ironbridge Gorge, near Telford. The county town of Shrewsbury still demonstrates its medieval past, and is intriguingly set on hills around which the River Severn winds.

I am delighted to present the reader with this photographic essay, after many jaunts into this region of diversity, whose features I believe are among the most interesting and stunningly beautiful in the whole of Britain.

Van Greaves

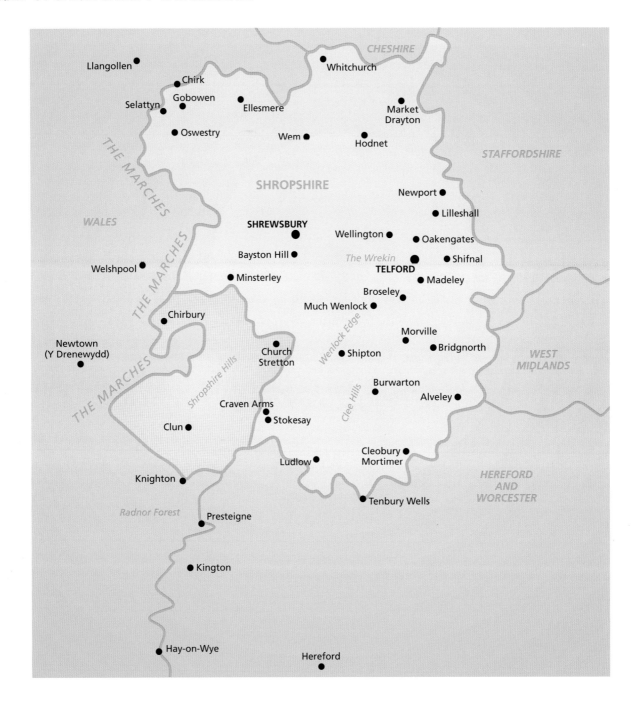

Sunrise over the Breiddon Hills from Stigwern Hill
The viewpoint on the hills between Newtown and Welshpool provided a striking vista looking east towards
the Breiddon Hills. Not only that, I had the bonus of a wonderful sun rising in just the right place.

The Dingle, Quarry Park, Shrewsbury
The wonderful colours in The Dingle gardens in Quarry Park, Shrewsbury, made this shot a justifiable inclusion.

Opposite: **Hodnet Hall**
This neo-Elizabethan mansion was built in 1870 to replace an earlier Tudor building. A visit is recommended, particularly to see the rhododendrons in the gardens. This shot places the house well in its man-made landscape.

Welshpool
We are looking down the main street of this busy Marches town, with Long Mountain providing the backcloth.

St Nicholas Church and Newport
This view of the congenial east Shropshire town is dominated by the sandstone tower
of the large parish church, which was extensively rebuilt in 1866.

Seventeenth-century building, Market Drayton
A close-up of period half-timbered architecture in the town centre of Market Drayton.

Market Hall, Bridgnorth
The focal point of High Town, Bridgnorth,
is the ancient Market Hall.

Patchwork Shropshire, from Cordon Hill
A typical Shropshire landscape, as seen from the hills above Clun.

Opposite: **Breiddon Hills and Rodney's Pillar near Arddlean**
The low, straight road between Welshpool and Oswestry provides a compelling foreground to the hills.

Cottage front, Claverley
The village of Claverley, east of Bridgnorth, stands on a hill and is well worth a visit both for its situation and its buildings, as seen here.

Raynald's Manor, Much Wenlock
The sign on this town centre building in
Much Wenlock conveniently gives its
date and original ownership.

River Severn and Bridgnorth
Seen from a point on the edge of Low Town, Bridgnorth looks more like a Tuscan hill town,
with its buildings and the parish church of High Town perched on the promontory.

River Severn, Rowing Club and Shrewsbury School
A shot which encapsulates the attractiveness of Shrewsbury's situation, built around the meanderings of the River Severn.

Clun Castle, the Keep
There was an Iron Age hillfort on this site, and the later Norman castle was simply accommodated within it.

Stokesay Castle
Claimed to be England's most perfectly preserved thirteenth-century manor house, Stokesay Castle,
now in the care of English Heritage, is reflected in the pond on an adjacent farm.

Stiperstones at sundown
Cranberry Rock and the summit rocks of the Stiperstones behind are captured in the dramatic light
of a February afternoon. The quartzite outcrops are around 480 million years old.

Opposite: **Long Mynd from Corndon Hill**
The feeling of the patchwork-quilt nature of the Shropshire landscape is again revealed
in this picture taken from Corndon Hill, looking towards the Long Mynd.

Long Mynd to Ragleth Hill
Early autumn colours begin to show in this view from the Long Mynd to Ragleth Hill. The village below is Little Stretton.

On Croft Ambrey Hillfort
Croft Ambrey is one of the major hillforts of the Marches. Dating from about 550BC, it is situated astride the southern end of the long ridge which runs from Bringewood Chase and High Vynnalls into Herefordshire.

Descending Cnwch Bank
This little known and seldom-visited hill country is contained between Radnor Forest
and Hay on Wye. Here, the photographer enjoys its solitude.

Towards Bryn Hill
The view is just east of Offa's Dyke and above Shadwell Hall, heading in the general direction of Bishop's Castle.

Ludlow Castle
A close-up study of this late-eleventh-century Norman castle originally built by Roger de Montgomery,
Earl of Shrewsbury, or Roger de Lacey. Ludlow Castle was especially favoured by the monarchy in early
Tudor times and is now the scene of regular Shakespearian productions.

Opposite: **Whittington Castle**
This picturesque spot, the gatehouse of a medieval castle, was once on the main A5 before the road was re-routed. It is a well-known
landmark which I passed on innumerable occasions on my way from the Midlands to Snowdonia for climbing weekends.

Old Bridge, River Wye, Hereford
The county town of Hereford is included as it comes into the region known as The Marches, a term
derived from the 'marches' or borders originally laid down by the Norman overlords.

Opposite: **Overlooking Cleobury Mortimer**
If I was trying to sell the town through a picture this would be it.
Old and new buildings alike blend in comfortably in an idyllic setting.

Shrewsbury and the River Severn from Shrewsbury School
Shrewsbury School was founded by Edward VI in 1552, and thus is one of England's oldest and most famous public schools.

Canoeists on River Severn, Ironbridge
This is the view downstream from the world's first iron bridge, built in 1779 over the River Severn by Abraham Darby,
and cast at his Coalbrookdale ironworks. The site is now part of a World Heritage Site.

Half-timbered house, Rushbury
Enhanced by the colourful *acer* tree, this three-gabled house is situated in Rushbury, a delightful hamlet on the slopes of Wenlock Edge.

Oswestry town centre
Llwyd Mansion, built in 1604 in Cross Street, Oswestry, is a fine timber-framed building in the centre of this border town.

Llanymynech Quarries

This nature reserve on Offa's Dyke Path, stands astride the borders of England and Wales. The limestone cliffs and scree slopes are important for wildflowers and insects, and the cliffs are a playground for the rock climber.

Opposite: **Caer Caradoc Hill from Cross Dyke, Long Mynd**

This winter shot was obtained on a day that 60 cars got stuck on The Mynd's narrow, hilly roads. I avoided that and was able to cross over the moor from Leebotwood on the A49 to Bridges. The hillfort on Caer Caradoc is said to be the last battleground of the Celtic leader Caractacus in his fight against the Roman invaders.

Acton Burnell Castle
This thirteenth-century fortified manor house was seat of Robert Burnell, chaplain to Edward I
and later Lord Chancellor and the Bishop of Bath and Wells. Despite the name, it is not really
a castle but an embattled manor house, now in the care of English Heritage.

Bridgnorth Castle
It is said the angle of the leaning keep of twelfth-century Bridgnorth Castle is greater than that of the Leaning Tower of Pisa.
It is the result of the Parliamentarians' attempt to blow it up in 1646.

Heath Mynd and Roundton Hill from Handless
Beautiful autumnal light in the foreground heralds two more of Shropshire's famous 'blue remembered hills'.

Offa's Dyke, Llanfair Hill
North of Knighton the dyke, built by Mercia's King Offa to mark his western boundary in the late eighth century, stands out boldly in the landscape. It is now the route of the 177-mile (283km) Offa's Dyke National Trail.

Abbot's House, Shrewsbury
The Abbot's House in Butcher Row, Shrewsbury is a fine example of a three-storey, pre-Reformation town house,
the ground floor of which is shops. It was often claimed to be the town house of the
abbots of Lilleshall Abbey, but this is not now thought to be the case.

Old Market, Shrewsbury
Another fine example of of Shrewsbury's historic architectural heritage is the Old Market buildings, seen here.

**Severn Valley
Railway operations**
A visit to the Bridgnorth railway sheds of
the famous restored Severn Valley Railway
enabled me to capture this picture.

Welshpool and Llanfair Light Railway
Another one for steam buffs, the Welshpool and Llanfair Light Railway is one of 'The Great Little Trains' of Wales.
Here an engine pulls out of the Welshpool terminus of the line.

Hydrangeas at Hergest Croft, Kington
These lovely gardens just to the west of the border
town of Kington, are well worth a visit.

Early purple orchid, Llanymynech Quarries
On the wilder side of things, this is the first orchid to appear among several varieties
to be found in early summer on the slopes of this fine nature reserve.

Towards Bridges and the Long Mynd
February snow etches out the features in the landscape in this wintry view from Stedment Farm.

Opposite: **Rock outcrops, Hergest Ridge**
West of Kington, this is another taste of Offa's Dyke country, looking towards Gladestry Hill.

Ellesmere Town Centre
Ellesmere lies at the centre of Shropshire's 'Lake District' – although the lakes
are very shallow and formed by hollows in the post-glacial drift.

Opposite: **Ludlow and Titterstone Clee Hill**
Surely one of the classic English town overlooks is this view of Ludlow
from Whitcliffe Common, to the west of the settlement.

Corner of Bull Street, Bishop's Castle
I've chosen what I think is arguably
the most photogenic corner of
this famous Shropshire town.

Lower Hall, Worfield
This privately-owned seventeenth-century dwelling was rendered in the eighteenth century, so covering the half-timbered structure. Thankfully the present owners have restored the façade to its former glory.

Montgomery overlook
This small border town is full of interesting buildings. The view takes in Corndon Hill beyond.

Spotlight on Knighton
Photographed in the same spirit as the previous picture, except the composition
is condensed with the sunlight highlighting a section of the town.

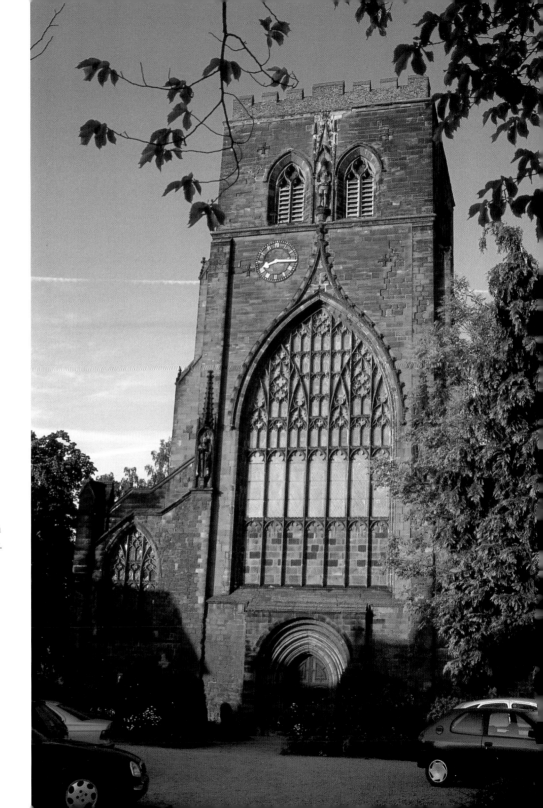

Opposite: **View of Croft Castle**
Winter light falls on this fine Georgian
Herefordshire house on the slopes beneath
the Croft Ambrey hillfort near Leominster.
The house is now in the care of
the National Trust.

Shrewsbury Abbey
Founded in 1083 as a Benedictine
monastery, Shrewsbury Abbey is
the setting for the popular *Cadfael*
mysteries by local author Ellis Peters.

Early light from Stigwern Hill
A dawn view from Stigwern Hill over the Rhiw Valley.

Opposite: **Paragliding from the Long Mynd, towards Corndon Hill**
The west scarp slope of the Long Mynd provides plenty of opportunity for followers of this modern adventure sport.

All Saints' Church, Little Stretton
Though only built within the last one hundred years, this charming church boasts
an original design featuring half timbering and a thatched roof.

Detached bell tower, St Peter's Church, Pembridge
This is one of the finest examples of a detached bell tower in the region.
Beyond is a glimpse of this Herefordshire 'black and white' village.

Brown Clee from Titterstone Clee
Decent compositions from the two Clee Hills – the highest points of Shropshire – are notoriously difficult to obtain.
This one taken from the summit rocks, however, seems to work reasonably well.

Opposite: **Last light from the Stiperstones**
A winter sunset gives the only feeling of warmth to the foreground of Cranberry Rocks. The Wrekin is seen to the left, and the other
flash of light could well be from the sun's reflection on the only remaining tower block on the skyline of Dudley in the Black Country.

Wem Mill
This Victorian mill at Wem is a listed
building no longer in its original use and
awaiting refurbishment into apartments.

Feathers Hotel frontage, Ludlow
A grade I listed building, the Feathers Hotel is one of the most famous and photographed buildings in Ludlow. The ornate black-and-white façade dates back to 1619. I have the never-to-be-forgotten privilege of dining and staying overnight here in a four poster bed for my honeymoon.

Clun

Clunton and Clunbury,
Clungunford and Clun,
Are the quietest places
Under the sun.

So runs the famous doggerel about the collection of Shropshire border villages, all of which take their names from the River Clun. This photograph shows the centre of the village of Clun.

The Green Man of Clun
The Green Man is a pagan symbol of the summer season. At May Bank Holiday, he rules the village,
seeing off the 'Frostie Queen' on Clun's bridge and thus heralding in the summer.
Festivities continue both in the village and in the castle grounds.

High Street, Church Stretton and Ragleth Hill
A picturesque autumn view from the High Street of Church Stretton, showing the hills,
including Ragleth, which give the little town its delightful setting.

Church Stretton and the Long Mynd from Ragleth Hill
The previous view in reverse, looking towards Church Stretton and the Long Mynd from Ragleth Hill,
and illustrating how the town gained its 'Little Switzerland' label.

Weobley, Herefordshire
Weobley is another of the classic 'black and white' villages of Herefordshire and The Marches.

Architecture in Presteigne
I chose this cameo shot of Presteigne, rather than struggle with a general view in the town.

Clun and the Clun Valley
A serene vista which shows the town of Clun and its castle to advantage.

Opposite: **Above Townhead Brook and the Devil's Mouth, Long Mynd**
The main characteristic of the Long Mynd is its numerous deep-cut valleys, known as 'batches',
which penetrate deep into the hills. They provide some lovely walks on to the moorland beyond.

Towards Whitton from Offa's Dyke Path
I think this photograph sums up the essential peaceful beauty of The Marches.

Opposite: **Shropshire Hills from The Wrekin**
Snow always adds an extra dimension to a view of the hills, as seen here from The Wrekin.

Bull Ring, Claverley
This village near Bridgnorth is well worth inspecting for its collection of interesting buildings.
The Bull Ring was used for bull-baiting in less civilised times.

High Street, Whitchurch
Whitchurch is a thriving north Shropshire town, caught here in a quieter moment.

Across the Pontcysyllte Aqueduct
This major feat of canal engineering towering across
the Vale of Llangollen is two hundred years old. If you
can cross it either in a barge or on foot avoiding
vertigo; good. If you can pronounce the name –
'Pont-ke-sethte' – even better!

Shropshire Union Canal, Hampton Bank
Literally, another quiet backwater on the Shropshire Union Canal.

Chirbury
A corner of the quiet village near Montgomery.

Darby House, Telford town centre
Blossom softens the modern architecture of Telford's new town centre.

Bradnor Hill and Herrock Hill from Hergest Ridge
Another autumn view, this time in Offa's Dyke country, west of Kington.

Opposite: **Caer Caradoc and The Wrekin from Ragleth Hill**
Two of Shropshire's fine hills are pictured here, enhanced by the rich colours of autumn.

River Severn and The Wrekin from Cressage
The Wrekin, Shropshire's iconic hill, is seen here from the B4380 road bridge over the river.
The hill is formed from the remnants of the plug of an ancient volcano.

Bridge over the River Clun at Clun
The medieval bridge at Clun acts as a focal point of the town. Its unusual saddleback
shape has five segmented arches and triangular breakwaters.

The Abyss, Grotto Area, Hawkstone Park
The figure in red (my wife), adds essential scale
to the most spectacular cliff in this park,
renowned for its follies and grottoes.

Offa's Dyke Path, Clun Hills
Another picture which oozes the serenity of The Marches. Figures in red, like this one, always contrast well with green backgrounds.

Pork Pie Shop and bent spire, Cleobury Mortimer
The shop has been in this business for a hundred years. The bent spire of St Mary the Virgin Church was described by Sir John Betjamin as 'having slipped out of place.' It was stabilised by Thomas Telford in the 1790s.

The Guildhall, Newport
This close-up reveals the date of the timber-framed, gabled building and its original owner.

Shropshire Canal at Blists Hill
Visitors to the Ironbridge Heritage Site who enjoy walking can do a circuit through the woods beyond
Blists Hill Victorian Museum, to see the inclined plane and return via the canal.

Opposite: **Ellesmere Lake**
The wooden duckboards provide a convenient angle to the composition, with the
added bonus of the fleet of Canada geese and boat beyond.

Ashes Hollow, Long Mynd
Another well-walked valley giving access to the
Long Mynd also provides numerous
photographic possibilities.

Opposite: **Moon over
Cranberry Rock, Stiperstones**
The rock on its own may not have been enough,
despite the late light. The figure and the moon
were included to add mystery.

Wilderhope Manor
This fine example of an Elizabethan manor house near Wenlock Edge has been a youth hostel for many years.
I well recall how it used to be freezing in the 1960s, but thank goodness, these days it is centrally heated.

Acton Round Hall
This fine, early-eighteenth century brick-built dower house to Aldenham Park is hidden away between the B4368 and the A458 beyond Morville. But it is well worth the short diversion.

View of Clunbury
A glimpse of one of the many Clun villages, 'quietest places under the sun', in the Clun Valley.

From Kerry Hills to the Breiddon Hills
The Breiddons jut out above Long Mountain, in this view from the Kerry Hills
shot on an indifferent day, with just enough interesting light.

Buildwas Abbey
Buildwas Abbey was a Cistercian monastery founded in 1135 beside the River Severn and
is not far from Ironbridge. These days it is an English Heritage site.

Opposite: **Wenlock Priory**
I tried a less-used angle on a well-photographed subject, situated in Much Wenlock. The Priory was of the
Cluniac order – nothing to do with the River Clun but one of the sister houses of the Abbey of Cluny in France.

Harley Dingle and Great Creigiau, Radnor Forest
This deep valley penetrates well into the confines of remote Radnor Forest.

Opposite: **Radnor Forest from The Warren**
The backlit sheep are beautifully spaced in an image obtained from the lonely hills between Kington and Presteigne.

On the Iron Bridge looking towards the town
Holy Trinity parish church, built in 1850–4 with money from the Darby family, dominates this view from the bridge.

Opposite: **Blists Hill Victorian Museum**
I was pleased that the smoke haze added some atmosphere to this shot of the horse and cart with
'Victorian' occupants, who are nicely balanced by the tourists on either side. Blists Hill is one
of no less than ten museums in the Ironbridge Gorge area, a World Heritage Site.

Hope Bowdler and Hope Bowdler Hill
This village between Wenlock Edge and the bulk of the Shropshire Hills
is well worth exploration. Hope Bowdler Hill rises behind the village.

Opposite: **St Chad's Church and the War Memorial seen from Quarry Park, Shrewsbury**
The open rotunda of Shrewsbury's War Memorial (1923) includes a statue of St Michael by A.G. Wyon.

Stiperstones from the Long Mynd
A wild aspect of Shropshire's hill country, taken from one of the moorland roads which traverse the hills.

Opposite: **Stiperstones summit silhouette**
Ask yourself what makes this picture. I think it it is the beautiful herringbone cloud filling
the top right of the image, without which it wouldn't have anything like the same impact.

From Wenlock Edge to the Shropshire Hills
This panoramic view was taken from the layby on the B4371 Much Wenlock to Church Stretton road, and reveals left to right,
Ragleth Hill, the Long Mynd, Caer Caradoc, more of the Mynd, the Lawley and the Stiperstones.

From The Warren to Brown Clee Hill
The compositional lines zigzagging from left to right up the picture are what
pleased me, and the cloud nicely balances the sky.

Spring in Eardisland, Herefordshire
This is yet another of Herefordshire's 'black and white' villages, beautifully situated
beside the River Arrow, which is seen in the foreground.

Wenlock Edge from Acton Scott
Note the tower, which is a folly, jutting from the tree-crested edge in the distance.

Opposite: **Bury Ditches hillfort**
Yet another of the large number of Iron Age hillforts
which dot the Shropshire and Marches landscape.
Bury Ditches is situated near Clun, and the Long
Mynd once again provides the backdrop.

Offa's Dyke, Edenhope Hill
Another undulating section of the Dyke
is illustrated here on Edenhope Hill,
with Corndon Hill on the skyline.

Daniel's Mill, near Bridgnorth
This corn mill is open to the public and the giant cast iron water wheel is still working.
It was manufactured in Coalbrookdale in the 1850s to replace a wooden one.

Opposite: **Power and pollution**
Seen from the Wrekin, cold winter air condenses the emissions from the CEGB power station, situated in the Ironbridge Gorge.

Radnor Forest from Beacon Hill
No matter from wherever the Radnor Forest is viewed, it always appears as a 'whaleback.' Beacon Hill
is a wild area over 500m in height to the north.

Winter aspect, Titterstone Clee Hill
Seen from near Stoke St Milborough, the second highest hill in Shropshire cuts a fine profile,
if you ignore the unfortunate collection of civil aviation radar masts on its summit.

Wroxeter, Roman city
The Roman name for Wroxeter was *Viroconium Cornoviorum*, taking its name from the local Iron Age tribe of the Cornovii. It was the fourth largest city in Roman Britain. The Wrekin, site of a Cornovii hillfort, watches over the scene in the background.

Opposite: **The approach to Chirk Castle**
This thirteenth century Marcher castle was built by Roger Mortimer for Edward I in the 1280s.
It commands a fine view across Cheshire towards the Pennines.

Otherworld: radar sphere, Titterstone Clee Hill
I carefully selected a viewpoint between the summit rocks to frame the most intriguing of the Space Age
air traffic control constructions which adorn the summit of one of Shropshire's highest hills.

Oak Tree Wall Direct, Pontesford Rocks
Pontesford Rocks is a former favourite
rock-climbing ground of mine. I returned
after many years' absence to obtain this
climbing photograph at the Earls Hill
Nature Reserve above Pontesford.

In Perkins Beach Dingle, Stiperstones
Two walkers climb this charmingly-named defile near Stiperstones village, heading for the main ridge above.
There are hints of storms over the Welsh mountains in the distance.

Opposite: **From Caer Caradoc towards The Lawley and The Wrekin**
Angular light picks out the rocks near the summit of Caer Caradoc. Caer Caradoc
is a mountain in miniature, and said to be the scene of Caractacus's last stand.

Black Mountains and Radnor Forest from Corndon Hill
Atmospheric clarity and strong evening light define this distant vista. Corndon Hill features
prolifically in this book, but it provides an obviously good viewpoint.

The Lawley from The Wilderness
A changeable day provided this picture. The Wilderness is accessible by a walk from nearby Cardington.

Little Wenlock from The Wrekin
The village of Little Wenlock is a useful starting point for a walking
circuit taking in Shropshire's landmark summit of The Wrekin.

Opposite: **Kington**
Kington is a Herefordshire town right on the Welsh border. Local weather proved
difficult for me on more than one photographic occasion.

Corndon Hill and Stiperstones from the Breiddon Hills
The walker looks over Long Mountain towards the Shropshire Hills on the skyline.

Breiddon Hills from Long Mountain
This shot looks back towards the previous picture's viewpoint, which was from the col between the two hills.

Berwyn Mountains from Long Mountain
Distant vistas with lots to see within a camera frame are something the purist photographer
is very careful about using. But the clarity of the air on this day made up for this.

The Whimble and Radnor Forest from Offa's Dyke, near Thorn
The thimble-shaped hill on the skyline is known as The Whimble. Though taken against the light, the picture seems to work.

Showjumping, Shrewsbury Flower Show
Every year, Quarry Park is the site of this famous flower show, which also boasts a number of other
attractions, such as showjumping. My visit was accompanied by typically unsettled British weather.

Opposite: **Shrewsbury Castle**
Roger de Montgomery's eleventh-century castle on a loop of the Severn is now a regimental museum,
as the guns in front suggest. Many additions were made between the twelfth and fourteenth centuries, including
the hall which dates from the reign of Edward I and which was heightened in the seventeenth century.

131

Compressor house, lead mine, Snailbeach
Life changes so rapidly in these days, but this short-lived industry on the northern end of the Stiperstones lasted a mere thirty years, closing for good in 1911.

The Knockin Shop

People may raise their eyebrows when you tell them you've been to 'The Knockin Shop'. The village of Knockin is north of Shrewsbury and west of the A5.

On Hergest Ridge with the Brecon Beacons beyond
This Marches' hill provides a fine view of the highest mountains in South Wales.

Opposite: **Devil's Chair, Stiperstones**
The story is that the Stiperstones were formed when the Devil spilt stones which he was carrying in his apron, intended for dumping in the valley and blocking the river. Instead, they ended up on the ridge. It is also said that if you spend midsummer's night here, you would return mad. The acute angle on the quartzite rocks and the wild sky add impact to the image.

The Iron Bridge, Ironbridge
The famous site has been photographed to death, but I hope this shot, dressed by blossom, does it credit.

Opposite: **Rail Car, Cliff Railway, Bridgnorth**
This is the oldest and steepest inland funicular railway in the country, built in 1892
and linking Low Town to this position at High Town.

Nordy Bank hillfort and Brown Clee Hill
This large Iron Age earthwork on Nordy Bank is perched half way up Brown Clee Hill.
Seeking a figure to add scale, I put myself in the picture.

Opposite: **Acton Scott Working Farm**
One of the shire horses being led out to pasture at this model farm, which depicts agricultural life as it was at the turn of the last century.

Llanymynech Quarries from the Shropshire Union Canal
Morning light shows the limestone quarries in relief from this currently-unnavigable
section of the Shropshire Union Canal.

Opposite: **Stiperstones from Corndon Hill**
Corndon Hill provides yet another grand aspect of the rugged Stiperstones.

RAF Cosford Aerospace Museum
The Fairey Delta 2 jet was flown by Peter Twiss to create a world speed record, and was the model on which Concorde's 'droop-snoot' nose was based. Beyond, note the TSR2, an aircraft in advance of its time but which never saw service due to cutbacks made by Harold Wilson's Labour Government. There is a Russian MIG 15 fighter, a Cold War adversary, on the right.

Gliding School, Long Mynd
Strong colour and compositional design lend intrigue to this image. The Midland Gliding Club which operates from
here was founded in 1934 and must have one of the most spectacular gliding launch sites in the country.

Titterstone Clee from Bitterley
I was running out of light and searching
for a view when I came across this field
of rich loam planted with fresh green
crops, whose lines led perfectly
to the turreted hill above.